Within the Trifles

Within the Trifles

Poems by

Marianne Brems

© 2025 Marianne Brems. All rights reserved.
This material may not be reproduced in any form, published,
reprinted, recorded, performed, broadcast,
rewritten or redistributed without
the explicit permission of Marianne Brems.
All such actions are strictly prohibited by law.

Cover design by Shay Culligan
Cover image by Behnam-Mohsenzadeh on Unsplash
Author photo by Joan Bresnan

ISBN: 978-1-63980-849-6

Kelsay Books
502 South 1040 East, A-119
American Fork, Utah 84003
Kelsaybooks.com

for Joan

Acknowledgments

Thank you to the following publications, in which versions of these poems previously appeared:

Academy of the Heart and Mind: "Never & Always"
Agapanthus Collective: "Smooth for Now," "Invertebrate"
The Big Windows Review: "Delicate Song"
The Broken Spine: "A Simple Union"
California Writers Club Vision and Verse I: "Chorus of Voices," "Circle of Opposites," "Peach Tree"
Cider Press Review: "Broken Yolk"
Dear O Deer!: "No Room," "Pause"
Flapper Press: "The Seventy Somethings," "Proud Monument," "I Like Your Hat"
La Scrittrice: "Her Effacement"
Lavender Review: "Just a Button and a Hole"
Little Leaf Literary Journal: "Dish of Orphans"
Macrame Literary Journal: "Symphony of Stillness"
Midnight Fawn Review: "It's Like That Sometimes"
Mused: "Her Effacement"
The Orchards Poetry Journal: "A Room Once Empty"
Right Hand Pointing: "Pants Without Pockets"
The Scop: "Less Left," "Reliability"
Selcouth Station: "Rita"
Soft Cartel: "Silence"
Symphonies of Imagination: "Ordinary Ways"
The Wise Owl: "The Kingdom of *Enough*"
Writer's Egg Magazine: "Her Effacement"

Also by Marianne Brems

Stepping Stones

In Its Own Time

Unsung Offerings

Sliver of Change

Contents

I. ORDER

A Coming Together	19
Everywhere Yet Nowhere	20
Neat Folds	21
On Staples	22
Pants Without Pockets	23
Reliability	24
Things Put Away	26
A Simple Union	28

II. CONNECTION

A Room Once Empty	31
Peach Tree	32
Marriage Deal	33
Good Intentions	34
I Like Your Hat	35
Looming Torment	36
Proud Monument	38
Whole Sand Dollar	39
No Room	40
Wedding Vows	42

III. HOPE

Dish of Orphans	45
It's Like That Sometimes	46

Junk Mail	48
Just a Button and a Hole	50
Shared Humanity	51

IV. UNEXCEPTIONAL EVENTS

Invertebrate	55
Never & Always	56
Laundry Day	57
Pause	58
Sculpture	59
Smells	60
Space for Wonder	61
The Kingdom of *Enough*	62
These Pillows and I	63
Within a Shadow	64

V. PEOPLE

Her Effacement	67
In Between	68
Outdoor Experiments	69
Rita	70
Smooth for Now	72
The Seventy Somethings	73
Morning After the Election	74
Five Friends	75
Less Left	76

VI. NATURE'S WAYS

Ordinary Ways	81
As Long as Destiny Allows	82
Chorus of Voices	83
Delicate Song	84
Moon	86
Pure Joy	87
Symphony of Stillness	88
Broken Yolk	89
The Binding of Things	90
Silence	91
With Purpose	92
Circle of Opposites	93

Trifles are the sum of life.
—Charles Dickens

I. ORDER

A Coming Together

Knitting speaks in
twists and loops and crossings over,
yarn turning this way and that
on needles bringing a web together
to make a scarf soft on the cheek.

String speaks of knots
in hard bunches,
taming two strands of a shoelace,
the ends of ribbons,
the mass of a pork tenderloin.

These twists, loops, crossings
of cotton, hemp, linen, wool,
join strands, ends, masses
in ways I wish could apply
to everyday ins and outs,
the ruffling and smoothing
of human interactions.

Everywhere Yet Nowhere

Without shape or color or texture
or any visible trail,
time races forward
without looking back.

It's everywhere yet nowhere,
as nano seconds pass
between ticks of the clock
and tiny deaths that occur every second
as hearts within stand still between beats,
then spring to life once more.

Such a miracle,
yet we spend hours in regret
that laundry's not done,
mail's in a heap,
we see too little of loved ones.

Neat Folds

Like a dessert before the first bite,
sheets in a clear package are perfect.
All corners meet at exact right angles
and they make a pleasing thump
when landing on the dresser.

But body motion, water, heat,
and rapid revolutions of the spin cycle
soon distort this symmetry.

When sheets billow from the dryer,
I give one a thwack.
A corner in each hand, I stretch my arms wide,
press my chin into the middle,
breathe in the scent of hot cotton,
fold,
bring corners together.
But hems run askew as corners
go where they will.

I long to tidy a precision off kilter,
make the energy of exactness mine,
within neat folds of Egyptian cotton
before they run free across my bed.

On Staples

A staple gains stature
by what it holds together.
Two tiny holes is the emptiness
that makes a bundle whole.
With the kachunk of a Swingline
some commonality
turns disparate things to one
with a definitive permanence,
a sweet closure,
often overlooked,
missing entirely with the noiseless glide
of a paper clip.

Pants Without Pockets

Pants without pockets
like doors without knobs.
No functional implement
to receive a key.
No access to a splendor within.
These dark deflated caves
to lodge coins or clover leaves
or hands in the cold,
with entrance and exit
conveniently the same,
homeless
without pants to thrive in.

Reliability

Early morning nightness,
most windows on my street still black,
the same few lit as always.

Traffic light changes.
Cars to the left and to the right stop.
Cars in front and behind move ahead. Repeat.

CalTrain #105 passes Menlo Park
mornings at 6:28 just ahead of me
on its reliable route to the city.

Steam rises through the dark from the pool.
We churn back and forth on the clock
in lanes of uniform length, constant width.

Then we rush through forty-degree dawn
to shower, change, get to work,
or take kids to school.

Reliability—the lynchpin of my morning
in a world where power goes out, storms disrupt, cancer intrudes,
all without warning.

Things Put Away

I put away dishes
when the dishwasher's done
so plates and forks
can fill their places on the table.

I empty hot sheets
from the dryer
so they'll bring sparkle
to an empty bed.

I hang up the leash
after walking the dog
and it's there in the morning
where I put it last night.

I only waste time searching for keys
I didn't put back,
time taken away from
sowing seeds in the earth.

I put away thoughts
pushing me where I don't want to go
to reach places where
only rain drops from the sky.

All is the movement
of things once taken out then put back,
the closing of one
for the opening of another.

It's the balance
of give and take,
the going then the coming
with sleeves rolled up.

A Simple Union

It's the coming together of two parts
in the grasp of a bolt and a nut
that eases a muscle fiber within,
tight with uncertainty
about the day ahead.

Something about this bolt
travelling smoothly across metal threads,
then locking against
a previously vagrant component
to join it with its other half
sets things right for a moment or two
in one simple unambiguous union.

II. CONNECTION

A Room Once Empty

To open the door for someone leaving
adds a dusting of affinity.

To pull out a chair to welcome a guest
draws two spirits into one.

To hold up a coat to see a person off
completes a circle of connection.

As if we had grown one more organ,
sensitive to a nascent internal hum,

these nuggets redirect blood,
settle into open hands,

alter the way dust falls
in a room once empty.

Peach Tree

I've looked after this tree for thirty years.
We're old friends.
When I climb up the ladder to pick peaches,
I whisper, *Thanks for sharing.*

Before my wife died and left me here alone,
she would pick peaches at their very sweetest
and give little bags to people who came by the house.
She knew just when they were at their very best.

Now it's just me and there's a lot of work to do,
what with the pruning, I get help with that now,
and the harvest and the squirrels and the leaves.
There's always something.

But I find answers in this tree.
It tells me anything I really need to know,
you know, about patience and survival,
and how to take what comes.

Now without my wife, things get jumbled.
Sometimes I even forget to take out the trash.
When this tree tips just a little and winks at me,
it helps me keep together.

So glad you could stop by.
Before you go,
I'll get my basket and pick you
some nice sweet peaches.

Marriage Deal

We share a glass of wine.
You drink from one side,
I drink from the other.
I say, *You take the last sip.*

Good Intentions

The letters I never wrote
still in me.
The strokes I never swam
still within.
The thanks I was too busy to give
still there.
The people I could have helped
but didn't look back
still linger.

My course regrettably diverted,
but as much a part
of good intentions
as the hands I've held
when something cracked
and no one else was there.

Unfulfilled but not forgotten,
my good intentions come
from a place of further good,
ready in their hunger
not to solve all
but to stretch for a moment in peace.

I Like Your Hat

We're walking down the street
on the way to meet friends.
He stops a stranger and says,
I like your hat. I've never seen one like that,
and they run on for minutes.
I stare at him, point to my watch, roll my eyes.
We're late again and I will have to apologize.

He asks for directions to a restaurant,
then begins with *We've always wanted to go there
because I've heard . . .,*
then he shares with someone I've never met
that my favorite food is shrimp.
Doesn't he know I prefer salmon?
Again I roll my eyes.

There were so many times.

Only six weeks from diagnosis until he was gone.
It hasn't been that long.

If only I could take back every one of those eye rolls.

Looming Torment

Our lives will be different in a day or three,
or whenever election results come in.
For now, heaviness settles into our bones
and vital organs with a weight
like a hurricane on its way.
It's the group dread,
the uncertainty of a capricious storm,
the enormity of people's choices.

But it's personal too,
like facing surgery without knowing
how much cancer is inside.
It's the waiting for weeks to get a date,
then waiting some more and some more
in a small space curtained off
from scurrying people in scrubs and Hokas,
seconds crawling by like hours
before wheels head into the oblivion
of the operating room.

Will a hurricane of apprehension
follow the opening of this body
or will a cold lump of fear
melt in relief?

In the grip of this election,
some eat Doritos for dinner
because they can't face cooking,
some walk the same hallways again and again,

many pull out chairs for others,
bring them coffee,
sit with them,
just to feel the fabric of a common thread
within a looming torment.

Proud Monument

A hundred-year-old blue oak
with cables holding up its aging limbs,
its roots sending cracks across the sidewalk
where I walk on my way to I don't remember where.

I pass for a fleeting moment
beneath the ferocious weight
of this proud monument
outlasting everyone on this street.

These branches with so many years inside them
remind me
that anything worth remembering
speaks in a soft ageless voice.

I want the drivers I see
and the people crossing the street,
to be careful, to last a long time.
I want their kids to turn out all right.

This blue oak stands proud,
its roots reaching under,
its branches stretching over,
blessing those who pass between.

Whole Sand Dollar

The lifeless exoskeleton of a sand dollar,
now the property of sun and wind and sand,
lies on a beach among scurrying sandpipers,
broken shells, worn driftwood, tangled seaweed.

It may break under the oblivious feet of walkers
or the rush of continuous waves,
elements of a never-ending fragmentation,
but for now, it is whole.

Once purple, ciliated, it lay among others
like cookies on the ocean floor.
Now smooth and bleached by sunlight,
it lies half hidden in sand now home.

To take it as my own,
whole and rare as a four-leaf clover,
would be theft,
a selfish denial of its intended place.

A thin sheet of water rolls in
over the five petalled pattern of this skeleton.
As water recedes it will, or not,
return this gem to its rightful owner.

No Room

She likes to look her best.
This hasn't changed.
She wears sleeves that puff at the shoulders,
tops that tie in a little bow at the neck
and have pockets in unexpected places,
blouses in warm colors that make her skin glow,
even underwear without seams that show.

She does this without thinking
like she always has.

A few men notice,
though she's not really trying,
and ask her to dinner at some casual place.
She likes the company,
the talk about favorite authors,
the grandkids' first vacation at the beach.

Some she likes,
but not the ones who want to come over after dinner.
Really, some of them are nice too, but the nerve!

He's been gone just three years.
She still thinks about the smell of his jacket,
the way he'd talk to birds in the morning,
start a conversation with anyone on the street,
listen when one of the kids needed help.

It's just the way things are now.
Maybe they always will be.
But for now, there's no more room.

Wedding Vows

An outdoor wedding with space to breathe is what I wanted.
It rained in the morning, but too late to change the venue
called The Lost Garden.
Of course everyone in this small gathering hopes for the best.

The minister, beads of sweat sprouting on his forehead,
says, *We are gathered here today to celebrate the union of* . . .
just as a small cluster of oak leaves above my head
releases some leftover raindrops that roll down my nose.

High heels sink into moist soil.
Cotton and silk cling to bodies sticky from humidity.
Will the cello be safe from a stray shower?
A lizard runs across my bare toes then vanishes in the grass.
I watch my almost-husband's four-year-old nephew
fiddle with buttons on his shirt with a fresh orange juice stain.

We push rings onto fingers enlarged from warmth,
perform our confirmation kiss, look at each other, linger.
His head cocks ever so slightly to one side,
as if something just clicked.
He takes in a breath perhaps to begin a question,
but his nephew grabs his hand and says,
I'll race you to the car.

III. HOPE

Dish of Orphans

A small dish where I place orphans sits in my kitchen—
a screw or a shiny clip or the back of an earring
for safe keeping until I find where it belongs.

Of course years go by and I never find where they go,
but each time I see my dish, I think, *Ah, a work in progress.*
There's movement in my life.

I could take an opposite view and think,
I have no need for more unfinished business.
Toss this junk that only takes up space.

But *no,* there is comfort
in making the world small for a moment,
a place where the back of an earring
waiting for its other half offers hope.

It's Like That Sometimes

I walk into a waiting room
where I've never been before
to see a doctor I don't know
who may tell me things
I don't want to hear.

I sit in a chair still warm
from the person before me.

We know sitting leaves warmth.
We have this in common with birds.
It's what makes eggs hatch.

What could have come to life
from within this stranger,
leaving for me the warmth
of some unlikely birth?

It keeps me company.
I'm not alone in a room
where everyone's consumed
by the swells of their own lives.

Without fanfare,
people share things unwittingly,
things like the smile that makes a difference.
It's like that sometimes.

Warmth travels into my core
until this new warmth
and my own become one.

I hope the doctor in the next room
brings them good news,
or at least not bad news.

Junk Mail

Nearly a lost experience
to find anything in my mailbox
that calls to me
as distinct and exquisitely human,
unique within the corridor of infinity.

I look through the tiny mailbox windows
of my neighbors,
some boxes stuffed with bright colors,
only a few empty,
and wonder if some distant writer
has pierced the walls of anonymity
of a fortunate recipient.

But, I think not.
I feel a sameness
with these neighbors I rarely see.
We are a community of strangers
who find validation outside of boxes,
in a kitchen or a library or on a sidewalk,

perhaps in a foyer with mailboxes.

I pledge to greet my co-dwellers often,
learn their interests,
their hobbies,
their pets' names,
so my familiar voice
might help scrub away drudgery
as junk mail passes through
their listless fingers.

Just a Button and a Hole

A small white button lies on the floor in my closet.
Which among these many clothes could have lost it?

So many untamed halves in so many colors
joined by the coming together
of a white button and a button hole just the right size,
trimmed in matching thread.

Could a white button like a silver star in a dark sky
draw onlookers from all corners,
complete a circle
as it passes through its special hole?

Could a people divided
like an unbuttoned waistband,
unable to fulfill their purpose,
come together with a button and a hole?

Even if the button came loose
and lay a while on the floor,
someone might discover it, sew it back on.
Even if threads didn't match precisely
or the hole wasn't quite right,
promise might linger for a little while.

Shared Humanity

In this unfamiliar country,
tongues make words
of different shapes
than those I know.

I walk along and feel compelled
to reach beyond their speech,
to outwardly acknowledge
a shared humanity with others,
but my mouth is a stranger
to these foreign contours.

My foot catches an edge of the sidewalk.
Next I know my face is against the sidewalk.
Blood oozes from my lip.
A passerby helps me up.
Another pulls tissues from a package
then gives me the rest,
smiles,
meets my eyes so urgency eases.

A meeting in gestures.
I can feel it down to my toes
even as I taste my own blood.

IV. UNEXCEPTIONAL EVENTS

Invertebrate

My poem lengthens and contracts
like an octopus,
an invertebrate able to squeeze through
small openings or fill large cavities.

My words inside their colorful bonnets
swell and subside
and trip over one another
as I attempt to give them spine.

The octopus arms of my poem
move autonomously,
reaching, flopping, in any direction
at any time.

I try to anchor these unruly appendages
with curved muscular words
that grip like suckers
as they explore, taste, manipulate.

When my poem cries out for bed,
arms tucked in under a sheet and blanket,
I kiss it goodnight
only to find an arm or two already slipped out.

Never & Always

Without talk of units
marking beginnings and endings,
minutes, hours, years,
time distils to never and always—
never, a perfect absence,
always, a constant presence—
two opposites
on a plain white canvas.

Lacking density
or weight
or possibility of compression,
we frame moments absent
or present
and maybe back again
depending on footprints
running through the backyard.

Laundry Day

A family of laundry out on a line,
a shirt discolored under the arms
next to a bra with frayed edges
next to mismatched children's socks
next to a sheet with a hole in the middle
next to a handkerchief
with the remains of a blood stain,
all vivid remnants of urgent lives
renewing themselves after a day's work
in the freshness of sun and wind
on laundry day.

Pause

When a pause steps forward,
a space opens up to breathe deeply,
put the rush of the day on hold
between two of the
eighty-seven thousand seconds in a day.

It's a chance to speculate
if a pond is green or blue
and what combination
of organisms, sunlight, fallen leaves
makes it so,
or why roses keep their shape
even when they land on earth,
why a baby's hands close around
objects that brush their palms.

But a pause is shy.
It's the shadow unnoticed
on an overcast day.
It will hide in the bottom of your shoe,
crawl between your toes
if you don't give it reason to emerge.

It must be loosened from its lodging,
encouraged to unfold,
so breathing may go forward
to open a hungry space.

Sculpture

To see the wonder of the night sky,
bury the light of day.
To hear the full resonance of a concerto,
tune out the color of the walls.
To feel the elegant flight of the long-billed curlew,
dismiss the blue horizon.
Just let go.

The superfluous simply plays around the edges,
dipping and swerving,
until we let sediment fall away.

In its absence, grace, beauty ring free
like a sculpture emerging
when we release all stone in the block
beyond the form we desire.

Smells

Unlike paint, an introvert,
whose colors need encouragement to mix,
paint fumes, though not visible,
are extroverts.
No inducement necessary.
No shaking.
No tumbling.
No stirring.
They eagerly join hands,
mingle,
rejoice,
and give impromptu birth
to new consummations of themselves
that puff and billow
and swallow with keen appetite
anything within reach.

Space for Wonder

Why do letters in the alphabet
follow the order they do?
Why does Wednesday come before Thursday,
peanut butter spread under the jelly,
or mothers cradle their babies on the left,
but so many of us drive on the right?

Such randomness calls for answers
in a world hungry for slots with labels
that order content in googlable ways,
slots with no room for the lightness of wonder.

If only slots had pockets, space could be there,
space between facts that chafe against one another,
space for breath to pass clear through,
space for the unexamined bending of trees,

space for things that make no sense,
space for words that refuse to rhyme,
space to let answers lie
to questions that need no reply.

The Kingdom of *Enough*

First among amounts to consider is *enough,*
enough with its shaded walkways,
clear pools, and cool breezes.

The question is always, *How much is enough?*
Is almost enough *enough* if you add just a little water?
Is too much *enough* if you scrape a little off the top?

Trickier still is that *enough* for me
will surely be too little or too much for you
and vice versa.

If we try to make it uniform,
one of us will be scraping
or the other adding water

and shaded walkways
will become avenues of illusion
without clear pools or cool breezes.

These Pillows and I

The fabric of the pillows on my sofa
wears through a little at a time.
Stuffing reveals itself slowly
over the months and years
that parallel the decline of my limbs.

But pillows are recoverable, replaceable.
There's a way back,
while arms and legs have just one chance
to make their mark.

Perhaps best that way
or I'd be chasing new parts
while autumn and anniversaries pass me by,
my pillows lying still like sleeping cats
without the company they desire.

Within a Shadow

Shelves in my refrigerator nearly empty.
But next to ruby succulent strawberries,
in the lonely shadow of dill pickles sliced the long way,
sits the last third of a jar of Kalamata Olives,
dark as midnight,
floating in a liquid the color of Cabernet,
elegant almond shapes
and plump meaty mass obscured.

No match for the urgency of strawberries,
ready to pierce through shadow,
steal center stage,
these olives from the Peloponnese Peninsula
with homely purple-brown skins
keep the punch of sundrenched earthy flavor
to themselves in a dark corner
only to exceed their expiration date,
never to reach tongues that could celebrate.

V. PEOPLE

Her Effacement

She bites into a cookie and apologizes for crumbs.
She regrets not remembering the dates I traveled.
She laments not calling me sooner.
Can I forgive her, she asks, for the lateness of her card?

She agrees that winter days shrink miserably short,
that tomatoes taste best in August, not July.
Her only insistence is she's a failure with plants,
yet she presents me, nurtured by her own loving hand,
zucchinis perfect in firmness and size
and strawberries succulent and soft.

Were she bossy or boorish or willing to impose,
I could dismiss her with a monster at my throat.
But this inflation of politeness,
this everlasting deference,
effacing her words line by kind line,
lets dozing creatures slumber.
Without leap or splendor or appetite,
dull sedation creeps idly over me.

In Between

He's too big to be strapped to his mother's chest,
too small to color with crayons.

Too old to stay put when set on the floor,
too young to name the number of beads.

Too curious to stick around for cuddles,
too young to realize the danger of *hot*.

Too old to eat only with help,
too young to eat all by himself.

Too big to fit into yesterday's clothes,
too small to put away his laundry.

Just right to laugh when lifted in the air.

Perfect to draw smiles from everywhere.

Curious to follow and see where the dog goes.

Eager to explore by mouth life's every shape.

Right on to take in whatever comes
without thought to cause or consequence.

Outdoor Experiments

In the shape of a bird,
she etches her mark on the world
in yellow chalk on an asphalt driveway.

She rolls a ball down a slide,
then scoots down to catch it
before it hits the ground.

She stands on the seat of a swing,
hair flying in her face,
as her father gently pushes her.

She tests her strength
jumping next to a log
before leaping over it.

She velcros her sneaker straps together,
then hops forward, feet as one,
arms flailing for balance.

Depth and diameter,
distance and weight,
equal endless adventure.

Rita

Parking meters,
still the soldiers of urban islands,
guarding identical squares
of oil spotted pavement for timeshare.

I hate them except when they're broken.
Then they make my day.
Shouldn't a small concrete rectangle
with no view
be free like the air we breathe?

I shove in my quarters
and instantly feel hurried.
I never think *Put in a few extra*
so I can take my time.
People without urgency
find other ways.

Instead, I think of Lovely Rita Meter Maid
with her little white book
and military cap
who could leave an envelope
on my windshield if I'm late,
though she must be past eighty by now.

It's the urban drivers' ritual
not to be dismissed by LCD screens,
credit card modules,
or phone app capacity.
To me, it's still Rita who gives the final nod.

Smooth for Now

Like the smoothness of refried beans
or soft serve ice cream,
their perfect skin firm and sleek
as they fill your order,
their smiles creasing only temporary folds
that spring back with the vigor of fresh elastic.

A quickness punctuates their movements
with an energy they never imagine will fade,
their minds full with
resistance to parental restrictions,
fear of not fitting in,
earning money for school.

We need them for their desire to serve,
for their swift agile response,
for their supple willing smiles
before they grow into heartbreak,
face the demands of child rearing,
struggle to make ends meet
that will loosen their skin,
leave uninvited crevasses
that only time will tell them really don't matter.

The Seventy Somethings

The frequency of malfunctions in the body
marks this decade.
They need not be large to nag and persist,

cataracts, arthritic knuckles, aching knees,
hearing loss, irritable bowels, shrinking height,
though of course Medicare is a beautiful thing.

But it's the interval of occurrence,
the piling up of small failures
that becomes the distraction I regret.

Gone is the surge of energy as muscles flex.
No snap back from a delivery of power,
only the sluggish recovery from the last good effort.

I dream of a time when muscles obeyed
and carried me forward without extra charge.
Never a second thought back then.

Now I breathe in so oxygen can sustain,
breathe out so there's room to breathe in again.
Repeat, then repeat.

No lifeboat on the horizon, no way to turn back,
just a seat on a train that rumbles on and on
but stops more frequently in this place and that.

Morning After the Election

At 7:30 AM a woman walks to the end of her driveway
and begins pulling up yard signs along the road
for the candidate who lost.
We look at each other.
Her eyes widen just a little.
I want to throw my arms around her,
but, of course, I can't.
Instead I say, *Thanks for putting these up.*
She looks down and says,
It's time to move forward.
Yes, I think, but a tourniquet locks my chest.

Five Friends

Everyone should have a circle five friends,

one to recognize and appreciate
the color of your eyes,

one to call when wind wails in the night
and claps of thunder quickly follow dry lightning,

one to remember when you went to the park
with their daughter since her best friend wouldn't go,

one to tell you the news
that someone you both love may not last the year,

one to reach for your tangled hands
when it's time to notice the lavender of lilacs.

Perhaps a sixth for good measure
when others are helping someone else.

Less Left

He insisted on aging in place.

So her routine unfolds.
Toilet him.
Wash him.
Dress him.
Comb his hair.
Take his vitals.
Feed him.
Next day repeat.

No *thanks* in his eyes.
No smile on his lips.
Few words from his mouth.

Just a worn track in the carpet
from kitchen to bedroom
and a rented metal bed
with adjustable height and tilt.

She struggles to help him out of bed
then onto the chair in the shower.
Her back hurts when lifting.
Her strength isn't what it once was.
She's already exhausted by noon.

I can get you more help, her daughter often says.

A caretaker comes twice a week
when she walks with friends,
but he complains,
says he doesn't like strangers around.

There's less left of them both than yesterday.
She knows this can't go on,
yet she keeps saying *no* to saying *no more*
as walls hum faintly with murmurs from the past.

She had wanted a retirement community.

VI. NATURE'S WAYS

Ordinary Ways

The sun does ordinary things,
like rise and set daily,
but what if it went down
just once in a while,
when falling in exhaustion
into the dark bed of the horizon,
or rose at random,
disgorging light that stays
only as long as its preference lingers.

This confiscation of reliable order
would knock down the door to chaos,
raise questions about the length of a day,
throw off the balance of Yin and Yang,
force uncertainty into the timing of sleep.

As long as regularity is the norm,
it's up to us to bless the miraculous
within ordinary ways.

As Long as Destiny Allows

Tufts of gray and white fur
lie next to the trail,
some clinging to leaves and twigs.
No blood, no gore, just fur.
Was the hunger of one stalker
so all-consuming as to leave
this little behind?

In this animal world
where death nourishes life,
lives are often compressed
as a life-or-death chase
terminates in a broken neck.

But this fur that lingers
makes me hope
the pursued escaped,
seized one chance, maybe more,
to bounce, leap, gallop
between shadows
in defiance of a natural law
for as long as destiny allows.

Chorus of Voices

So many voices calling in a chorus
from sandstone tafoni mouths
clustered on a cliff
that rises from a turbulent sea.

Luring us like sirens
to hear the message they sing.
Is it a warning of dangers below?
Listen and you will know.

Or do they summon passing birds
to rest within their cavities,
sheltered from wind and rain?
Listen and you will know.

Or is this a celebration of moisture, wind, salt,
mouths huddled together in unison,
and the sun that blesses it all?
Listen and you will know.

Delicate Song

A gray-brown wren
not much bigger than a shallot
lays sticks, leaves, grass, moss
between the discharge port
and the starter recoil of a lawnmower,
it's spinning blades
and choking exhaust
idle for now.

On the red metal chassis
of this cutting machine,
a home now waits for offspring
to emerge from eggs
the size of marbles
that will face dangers
as great as the killer blades below.

This mother wren
will leave her nest
to hunt and gather
while predators lurk,
paws may crush,
blades might cut.

But her tiny beak
despite the raiding of her nest
or a labyrinth of other dangers
will free a larger currency
anywhere she goes
through the miracle
of sweet notes
within her delicate song.

Moon

A white slice thinly
riding on water
mirroring every ripple
on an ever-changing stage.
The moon so easily bends.

Pure Joy

A thin sheet of salt water,
with a froth of bursting bubbles
lies spent on a smooth bed of sand
long enough for two small pairs of feet,
tentative against the cold,
to pierce its perfect surface.

Two slender bodies jump and skip,
clasp hands as they follow
the water receding rapidly,
gathering into a wall.
Just as the peak tips onto itself,
they turn and run.

Foam spills over them,
as they gasp, shriek,
and tumble against one another
in a bubbling white turbulence.

They sputter, giggle,
and regain their footing,
fling handfuls of water
into the air and at each other
without thought to the sun's burning rays
or sand that will later get in their shoes.

Symphony of Stillness

From three hundred sixty degrees,
a symphony of stillness emerges,
one that quiets the rustling
of moments jostling against one another,
one whose bars settle over sound,
one whose rhythm matches a heartbeat.

In this orchestra,
the settling of pollen plays bass,
the flight of a gull, bassoon,
the unfolding of crimson columbine, piccolo,
the ruffling of foxtail, horn.

The sudden hum of a hungry bee
that swells and recedes
along its winding course in search of nectar
further grows this *stillness*
with a song all its own.

Broken Yolk

I notice a small nest
on the casing around my porch light
protected under the eaves from rain.
My four-year-old niece sees a small bird nearby.
Later we see a tiny broken egg yolk and bits of shell
lying on the porch under the nest.

My niece says, *What's that?*
It's an egg from the nest, I say.
She looks hard at the egg, then the nest.
Why isn't it in the nest?
I'm not sure what to say.
Sometimes things happen we don't like, I respond.

As we go in the house, she looks back.
We get out things for lunch.
After we eat she draws with crayons—
a lot of blue sky, the brown mess of maybe a nest,
a bird's head far from something yellow, perhaps a yolk.

Should we bury it? she asks.

I know then she knows what I know.

The Binding of Things

In foolish haste
I bind things together with
nails, screws, tape, cement
to hold them solidly
because I want them so.

Better that things should go
as they will
like a scar bringing together
the edges of a wound
to make skin whole again,
raised, darker, proud.

Or bones that fracture
yet with time and granulation
grow whole again,
comfortable and secure
in their function as structure.

Best is when two minds
stumble and collide in a headwind
then bind like two shapes
coming together in the
blending of clouds
on a mostly clear day.

Silence

Silence is a hole to be filled,
or not filled
in a personal hive of pockets.

Sound is the filler
that occupies the hole
like salt in a cellar.

Silence is the vessel
that holds the sound
folded in its arms,
or nestles, satisfied
to feel the quiet
of a lone fish in a deep pool.

With Purpose

Legs blur
as bandy-legged sandpipers speed across wet sand
gobbling up worms, shrimp, small crabs
exposed by receding waves.

No time to waste.
Summer feathers beginning their molt.
Fall-winter plumage of greyish-brown coming in.
Outer wing feathers primed for the long journey south.

Thousands of miles in wind, calm, storm
with brief stops in Quill Lakes, the Bay of Fundy,
or Delaware Bay where hundreds of thousands feed
for a week or two as their body weight doubles.

No bags, no maps, just an inner compass.
Hundreds gather on the sand, poised, ready.
Finally, in a symphony of wing beats,
they lift with common purpose into the mist.

Circle of Opposites

The cormorant and its reflection,
their dark wingtips nearly touching,
a circle of opposites
silhouetted in the early morning sun.

One half
a bold aggressive warrior
with muscular wings and hooked beak
built to plunge for food
and snatch struggling prey.

The other half
without heart or lungs
or appetite for fish and crabs,
just a fragile mirror image
dissipating instantly in the slightest breeze.

About the Author

Marianne Brems has an M.A. in Creative Writing from San Francisco State University. She is a long-time writer of nonfiction, and her publications include textbooks in her teaching area of English as a Second Language and several trade books.

She began writing poetry in mid-life to capture essence and order in random events of daily life. She has a special interest in writing poems that examine curious aspects of the physical world. She is the author of the collection *Stepping Stones* (Kelsay Books, 2024) and the chapbooks *In Its Own Time, Unsung Offerings,* and *Sliver of Change.* Her poems have also appeared in many literary journals.

She lives in Northern California where she loves to cycle, hike, and swim.

Website:
www.mariannebrems.com

www.ingramcontent.com/pod-product-compliance
Lightning Source LLC
Chambersburg PA
CBHW060839190426
43197CB00040B/2706